SALVATION
(ARE YOU REALLY SAVED?)

APOSTLE EMMANUEL A. ADJEI

SALVATION

(ARE YOU REALLY SAVED?)

By

Apostle. Emmanuel. A. Adjei

Copyright ©2020 by E. A. Adjei

All rights reserved.

ISBN: 9798652295134

Write to:

Apostle Emmanuel A. Adjei

fofo275@hotmail.com

This book is dedicated to
Bishop Richard Aryee

Bishop Richard Aryee is my father in the Lord sent to me through Bishop Dag Heward-Mills.

My association with Bishop Aryee has been a message of blessing, inspiration, humility, the fear of the Lord and wisdom to me from him. It has been a message of strength, understanding, love and faith. Among many things that I have learnt and am still learning from bishop is that it is far possible to be that which Christ wants us to be. His life itself ministers to me as a pastor. His words are anointed to me and I am blessed to have him as a father in the Lord.

CONTENTS

INTRODUCTION 5

SALVATION IS GOD'S MAIN PURPOSE AND ONLY
PRIORITY 7

WHY WE SHOULD LOOK AT THE ISSUE OF SALVATION ... 9

THINGS THAT MANY CONISDER TO BE SALVATION 11

WHAT IS SALVATION? 22

HOW DO YOU BECOME SAVED / A CHRISTIAN / A
BELIEVER? 26

IS IT ONCE SAVED FOREVER SAVED? 32

THE ATTITUDE A PERSON MUST HAVE REGARDING
SALVATION 39

INTRODUCTION

God's interest in humans is not necessarily the same as our interest. His interests are not necessarily our cars, marriages, careers…etc. God's main interest in humans is their salvation. The cars, the homes, the marriages…etc, are things that God will help us obtain because we need them, but His priority is our salvation.

Remember when King David, King Solomon and others were alive? There were no cars, but they were blessed. There were no aeroplanes and shopping malls, but they were blessed. So, God's interest for you is salvation. On earth God is not doing anything apart from salvation. All other things are an addition - never forget that. This is one of the reasons why Christians have challenges because, most of the time, God's priority is not their priority. Some even think that they are doing God a favour by going to church or becoming a Christian. We can see this by their attitude, so we must understand that God's main purpose for mankind - for you - is salvation. For God's way to be had, whatever needs to happen for you to be saved God will surely do so. David said, may I not be rich so that I forget you and say I do not need you, nor may I be poor so that I will need to steal and do evil to survive; only let me be okay, so that I may serve you. He understood that riches could affect his salvation, as can poverty. King David was simply saying that he wanted to be in a state where he would be saved at the end of the day…and that is God's plan for us.

"Two things I ask of you, Lord; do not refuse me before I die: Keep falsehood and lies far from me; give me neither poverty nor riches but give me only my daily bread. Otherwise, I may have too much and disown you and say, 'Who is the Lord?' Or I may become poor and steal, and so dishonor the name of my God."

Proverbs 30:7-9

SALVATION IS GOD'S MAIN PURPOSE AND ONLY PRIORITY

Jesus said, in *Mark 8:36-37,* that what shall it profit a man if he gains the whole world and loses his soul. By this statement Jesus was saying that as far as He, and God, are concerned, nothing is worth more than salvation or to cause one not to be saved. In other words, His priority for you is that you will be saved. He has not prioritised your earthly things above your salvation and He has explained why, by saying that salvation cannot be bought with anything on earth. It is too precious and expensive, and it cannot be purchased. There is nothing you can give in exchange for your soul. It is not a commodity to be sold and that is why many people will not be saved.

What good is it for someone to gain the whole world, yet forfeit their soul? Or what can anyone give in exchange for their soul

Mark 8:36-37

Nothing is worth more than salvation. There is a scripture that says that even if your eyes prevent you from being saved, then you must uproot your eye. How much more marriage, your job, sex, finances…etc. You must understand that with God, His interest is your salvation. Other things are merely additions.

If your right eye causes you to stumble, gouge it out and throw it away. It is better for you to lose one part of your body than for your whole body to be thrown into hell. And if your right hand causes you to stumble, cut it off and throw it away. It is better for you to lose one part of your body than for your whole body to go into hell.

Matthew 5:29-30

Salvation being Gods main interest for you, is why, in *Matthew 6* Jesus said to seek first the kingdom of God and its righteousness, and then, He went on to say, all other things that you want and that He wants for you, would follow. The key is to seek the kingdom of God - which is salvation first. This means that the kingdom of God (salvation) must be your priority. The Bible's map for blessings from God is to seek God and His righteousness first. So you must understand that God's heart, purpose, plan and priority for you first and foremost is for you to be saved and that you will find His kingdom and righteousness (salvation) as you seek.

When God looks at you, He does not think of anything other than your salvation first and foremost because that is what you cannot buy and that is the real jewel.

For the pagans run after all these things, and your heavenly Father knows that you need them. But seek first his kingdom and his righteousness, and all these things will be given to you as well.

Matthew 6:32-33

WHY SHOULD ONE LOOK AT THE ISSUE OF SALVATION?

One of the reasons why it is important that we examine the subject of salvation is that in *2 Corinthians 13:5,* as well as other scriptures, it is highlighted that whether we are saved (in the faith) or not we must make it a priority to examine ourselves whether we remain saved.

Examine yourselves to see whether you are in the faith; test yourselves. Do you not realize that Christ Jesus is in you—unless, of course, you fail the test?

2 Corinthians 13:5

The scripture above says that we should test ourselves to know whether we are in the faith. As you are in the faith, so you can come out of the faith. Being in the faith means that you are saved. The scripture tells us that we as individuals must examine ourselves because, only we can do that. If you test yourself you will know whether Christ is in you or not, or whether you are saved or not. We are therefore supposed to examine and test ourselves to determine if we are saved and if we are still saved. No matter what, every now and then you must reflect on your actions – familiarity can set in and we can take the things of God for granted as they begin to become ritual. You can begin to trust in yourself and drift from God. People do not just drift from

God suddenly. You drift slowly and it may take years to realise that you have backslidden. Hence, the subject of salvation is not only for the unsaved but also for those who are saved. Therefore, God has asked me to write this book– it is vital that we understand what salvation is.

THINGS THAT MANY CONISDER TO BE SALVATION

In this life many people have mixed things up and this is one of the challenges. For example, when it comes to marriage many have confused things. The underlying reason for marrying should be because of love but many people have mixed it up with money and many other things. People now get into marriage because of things other than love and they later want the love to be present. Unfortunately, they cannot get this love that they now desire because there was no love in the mix to begin with or they simply loved other things. In this same way, when it comes to salvation, many have mixed it with many other things, but salvation is SALVATION. Salvation is not prayer, salvation is not miracles, salvation is not the Holy Spirit, salvation is not the power of the Holy Spirit, salvation is not attending church. Salvation is SALVATION. Salvation is not "I know God" and salvation is not fasting. So, what is salvation? We must really understand what salvation is. Before we can look at what salvation is, I want to mention a few things that many times people mistake to be salvation.

RICHES / PROSPERITY

Many people confuse riches or prosperity on earth to be salvation. Of course, saved people do become rich and prosperous but many people confuse prosperity to mean that a person is blessed of God, meaning that he or she is saved. Prosperity is not salvation. Many of the very rich people of this earth do not even accept God, they worship idols. In the church it sometimes comes across that prosperity is equated to salvation, which is not correct. We must understand that prosperity is not salvation. We should not mix it. In *Luke 16* Jesus tells us of a rich man and a poor man who died; however, the poor man went to heaven/paradise and the rich man went to hades/hell. While they were on earth it looked as though the rich man was the one who was blessed, but rather it was the poor man who was saved. It does not mean that rich men cannot be saved - many will be saved - but you cannot take success, riches, and prosperity to be an indication of salvation. You will notice in *Luke 16* that the rich man did not make it to heaven. It is easy for many people to think that the more they prosper and the more success they enjoy it must mean that they are saved. No, it does not mean that they are saved even though saved people can also be – and often are - prosperous and successful, but we cannot equate blessings, prosperity or success as salvation or as marks that a person is saved.

There was a rich man who was dressed in purple and fine linen and lived in luxury every day. At his gate was laid a

beggar named Lazarus, covered with sores and longing to eat what fell from the rich man's table. Even the dogs came and licked his sores. "The time came when the beggar died and the angels carried him to Abraham's side. The rich man also died and was buried. In Hades, where he was in torment, he looked up and saw Abraham far away, with Lazarus by his side."

Luke 16:19-23

and constant friction between people of corrupt mind, who have been robbed of the truth and who think that godliness is a means to financial gain.

1 Timothy 6:5

PRAYER

As a pastor, when I ask people the question of whether they are saved or whether they have accepted Christ Jesus as their Lord and personal Saviour, they normally answer that they pray all the time and therefore are with God. Many equate this scenario as evidence that they are saved or have obtained salvation. Prayer is not salvation. No matter how many times one prays it does not mean that they are saved. Wicked people can pray, as can unbelievers. Of course, those who are saved also pray but you cannot equate prayer to salvation. There are religions where they pray three, and five times a day, but they are not saved.

In *Proverbs 28:9* the scripture tells us that when an evil person or one who is in disobedience to God prays, their prayers are an abomination to God; this makes it clear that we cannot equate prayer to salvation. We are also told that anyone who does not obey the word of God, that person's prayer is detestable to Him, meaning that God hates their prayers. You cannot live in disobedience and assume or think that because you pray you are saved. That fact that you are prayerful does not necessarily means that you are saved, even though, as we have said, saved people do pray.

If anyone turns a deaf ear to my instruction, even their prayers are detestable.

Proverbs 28:9

"Not everyone who says to me, 'Lord, Lord,' will enter the kingdom of heaven, but only the one who does the will of my Father who is in heaven.

Matthew 7:21

SIGNS / WONDERS / MIRACLES / POWER

Signs, wonders, miracles, and manifestations of power are not salvation. The Bible says that the gifts and the calling of God are irrevocable. When God gives you gifts, He will not take them back, but this does not mean that you are saved, because you can lose your salvation. Working miracles, performing signs and wonders and demonstration of power, cannot be equated to salvation. These manifestations of power do not automatically mean that that person is saved even though saved people do and will perform miracles, signs and wonders and exhibit the power of the Holy Spirit. This also applies to the one who is receiving the miracle and the signs and wonders. You cannot say that because you have experienced or received a miracle or performed miracles, signs, and wonders, that you are saved because salvation is SALVATION.

In *Matthew 7,* Jesus said that there were people who prophesied in His name, cast out devils in His name, preached the gospel in His name but ultimately, He said that He did not know them! Meaning all along there were not saved. As a matter of fact, Jesus said that the people were evil doers, workers of iniquity and told them to get away from Him. To be away from Christ means to be with Satan. It is therefore a truly dangerous thing to equate the power of the Holy Spirit, as salvation. In *Luke 13:27-28,* the bible says that evildoers will go to hell meaning they are not saved.

"Not everyone who says to me, 'Lord, Lord,' will enter the kingdom of heaven, but only the one who does the will of my Father who is in heaven. Many will say to me on that day, 'Lord, Lord, did we not prophesy in your name and in your name drive out demons and in your name perform many miracles?' Then I will tell them plainly, 'I never knew you. Away from me, you evildoers!'

Matthew 7:21-23

But he will reply, 'I don't know you or where you come from. Away from me, all you evildoers! "There will be weeping there, and gnashing of teeth, when you see Abraham, Isaac and Jacob and all the prophets in the kingdom of God, but you yourselves thrown out.

Luke 13:27-28

PROFESSING TO BE CHRISTIAN

The fact that you say you are a Christian does not make you one or mean that you are. The above scripture says that many people will say "Lord, Lord," but will not enter the kingdom of God, neither will they be saved. This means that there are many people who say things like "God, God" or, "I am a Christian, God is good, God has blessed us," but they are not saved. The fact that they say that does not mean that they are saved. This salvation issue is important because it can be mixed up. Many people profess to be Christians, many people say things like, "God is there; I love God; if it had not been for God; it's the mercy of God…etc," but that does not mean that they are saved. The fact that they say and portray these things is not proof of their salvation, although saved people do make such statements. Jesus Christ Himself said this…

Not everyone who says to me, 'Lord, Lord,' will enter the kingdom of heaven, but only the one who does the will of my Father who is in heaven.

Matthew 7:21

All the above makes the issue of what salvation is very important because you can mistake a lot of things for salvation.

HOW LONG ONE HAS BEEN IN CHURCH DOES NOT DETERMINE SALVATION

How long ago you first received Christ as your Saviour, the length of time you have been in the church or whether you were born into a Christian family; these things do not mean you are saved. You are not saved because of how long you have been in the church, how long you first accepted Christ as your Saviour or because you were born into a Christian family. If that was the case, then *2 Corinthians 13:15* would not ask us to examine and test ourselves on whether we are still in the faith. Why would the Bible ask us to do this? It is because people can and do backslide and people can grow from walking with God to falling away when it comes to their salvation.

Examine yourselves to see whether you are in the faith; test yourselves. Do you not realize that Christ Jesus is in you—unless, of course, you fail the test?

2 Corinthians 13:5

In *Matthew 25:1* Jesus said that the kingdom of God will be like ten virgins that went out to meet the bridegroom. The bridegroom is Jesus. They were classified as ten virgins because they were considered pure. Verses *10-13* of the same chapter speak about salvation; we are told that there were ten virgins, that they were all pure and that they were all waiting for the coming of the Lord. Now there are two ways that we will experience the coming of the Lord. Either we will be alive when He comes, or we will die and meet Him where He is. Therefore no one knows their hour, so must therefore be prepared at all times. The scripture says that when their hour came, which was the coming of the Lord, five were not ready because they had left the house (symbolic for salvation). They were in the house before (they were saved, in Christ) but at the time of the coming of the Lord they had gone out of the house (were now backslidden). This can also be understood as meaning that they were in Christ, but that they then went out of Christ. When the Lord came, He told them that they could no longer enter because it was the state of their *current* state at that moment that determines who's they were and where they belonged – *not* their past position. If that were the case, then actually, no one would be considered saved because we were all once sinners! It is only when you repent that you can qualify as saved. So, how long you have been saved does not matter - it is your *present* state that matters. It is easy for people to 'play' church, to 'behave' like a Christian, and go around under the false pretence that they are saved. Doing these things does not determine your salvation or mean that you are saved…you can easily begin to backslide.

At that time the kingdom of heaven will be like ten virgins who took their lamps and went out to meet the bridegroom.

Matthew 25:1

"But while they were on their way to buy the oil, the bridegroom arrived. The virgins who were ready went in with him to the wedding banquet. And the door was shut. "Later the others also came. 'Lord, Lord,' they said,

'open the door for us!' "But he replied, 'Truly I tell you, I don't know you.' "Therefore keep watch, because you do not know the day or the hour."

Matthew 25:10-13

Once the owner of the house gets up and closes the door, you will stand outside knocking and pleading, 'Sir, open the door for us. "But he will answer, 'I don't know you or where you come from. "Then you will say, 'We ate and drank with you, and you taught in our streets. "But he will reply, 'I don't know you or where you come from. Away from me, all you evildoers! "There will be weeping there, and gnashing of teeth, when you see Abraham, Isaac and Jacob and all the prophets in the kingdom of God, but you yourselves thrown out.

Luke 13:25-28

These are some of the very basic things that many people mix up and confuse with salvation. Being a pastor does not mean that you are saved even though pastors are meant to be saved people and, of course, many are indeed saved. Being a church member does not make you saved either, even though clearly, saved people are church members and do go to church.

WHAT IS SALVATION?

What is salvation or what does it mean to be saved? When we say salvation, we mean one who is a Christian or a disciple of Christ Jesus. It is those who are saved whom we call Christians or disciples of Christ Jesus. The word Christian, believer or disciple of Christ Jesus are words which are used for people who are truly saved.

What is salvation?

In *Acts 11:25-26,* the disciples of Christ Jesus were called Christians. This indicates that a Christian is a disciple of Christ Jesus. When we say a Christian, it's not a label or an inheritance but we mean that the person is a disciple of Christ Jesus. The word 'disciple' means a follower. This implies that a Christian is a follower (disciple) of Christ Jesus.

Then Barnabas went to Tarsus to look for Saul, and when he found him, he brought him to Antioch. So for a whole year Barnabas and Saul met with the church and taught great numbers of people. The disciples were called Christians first at Antioch.

Acts 11:25-26

It is a disciple of Christ Jesus who is saved. It is those who are disciples of Christ Jesus who have salvation. They are the people who are Christians or are called Christians. Who is a disciple (follower) of Christ Jesus? In *John 8:30-31* the scripture tells us that it is those who hold on to the teachings of Christ Jesus who are really His disciples; not those who have knowledge of His teachings or are able to teach His teachings – but only those who do His teachings are the true disciples.

Even as he spoke, many believed in him. To the Jews who had believed him, Jesus said, "If you hold to my teaching, you are really my disciples."

John 8:30-31

Now the Bible says that a Jew is not of the flesh but of the spirit.

A person is not a Jew who is one only outwardly, nor is circumcision merely outward and physical. No, a person is a Jew who is one inwardly; and circumcision is circumcision of the heart, by the Spirit, not by the written code. Such a person's praise is not from other people, but from God.

Romans 2:28-29

From John 8:30-31 above, we learn that Jesus is saying that a disciple, or a Christian, is one who holds on to the teachings of Christ, one who is living in obedience to his word.

So a Christian or a disciple is one who is holding on (is obedient) to the word of God. This is what makes you a disciple of Christ. It is easy to think that you are a real disciple, but the reality is that you may not actually be one. It is easy to think that a metal with the appearance of gold is real gold, when actually it may be a counterfeit. Where is Jesus today for us to hold on to his Teachings? He is the Bible. The Bible is Jesus's entire teachings; as *John 1* says, 'in the beginning was the word and the word was God and this word that was God came to dwell amongst as Jesus Christ.' *Revelation* also tells us that Jesus' name is 'the word of God…'

In the beginning was the Word, and the Word was with God, and the Word was God.

*** John 1:1***

The Word became flesh and made his dwelling among us. We have seen his glory, the glory of the one and only Son, who came from the Father, full of grace and truth.

John 1:14

He is dressed in a robe dipped in blood, and his name is the Word of God.

Revelation 19:13

The one who holds on to the word of God (the Bible) is the one who is a Christian. A Christian is not a church goer, neither is a saved person the one who goes to church (even though a saved person or a Christian must of course go to church, as commanded by the word of God, which tells us not to forsake the gathering of the saints.) However, as we have seen, going to church does not make you saved.

Jeremiah 7:23 says that the people of God, Christians, or saved people are those who obey God's commands. In this scripture, the Lord says that if we obey Him, He will be our

God and we will be His people. This is exactly what Jesus said in *John 8*. If obeying God makes us His people (Christians, saved) then surely it is clear that not obeying Him makes us *not* his people (unsaved).

but I gave them this command: Obey me, and I will be your God and you will be my people. Walk in obedience to all I command you, that it may go well with you.

Jeremiah 7:23

A saved person or a Christian is one who obeys the word of God. A saved person is one who lives in obedience to the word of God. In other words, a Christian or a believer is one who is living in obedience to the word of God, not in previous obedience but one who *is* walking in obedience to the word of God. Obedience is ongoing. It sounds simple and indeed it *is* simple, but many have mixed it up and complicated it. One who is really saved is one who is holding on to the teachings of God and obeying the word of God. Everything I do as a Christian is because the Bible says I should and the things that I refrain from doing as a Christian are those which the Bible says I should not do. The one that I am following and the one that I am a disciple of instructs me on what I should and should not do. This is what makes me a Christian, a follower of Christ.

HOW DO YOU BECOME SAVED / A CHRISTIAN / A BELIEVER?

Salvation or being saved does not just happen. There is a clear path that God requires one to follow in order to be saved. There is a way to be saved. An individual can be in the church or born in a Christian family but if he or she does not do what needs to be done then they might not be saved. Let us be mindful that a saved person is one who is obedient to the Bible and the Bible teaches us what must be done to attain salvation. What are the main things that are required for us to be saved?

To be saved you must first repent and believe that Christ Jesus died and was resurrected. You must also confess with your mouth that you have accepted Jesus as your Lord and personal Saviour, you must be baptised in water, you must receive the Holy Spirit and you must continue in the Lord.

In *Acts 2:37-38* the scriptures say that when the people heard about the message of salvation, they wanted to be saved so they asked a direct question - "what shall we do to be saved?" So it is clear that there is something you must do to be saved; there is a way to be saved.

The scriptures plainly state that for one to be saved he or she must **1. Repent, 2. Be Baptised and 3. Receive the Holy Spirit**. The scriptures also explain why these three things are important. We are told that it was for the forgiveness of sin. This means that you cannot just wake up one day and say that you are saved. In this scripture three important steps were given regarding salvation…

When the people heard this, they were cut to the heart and said to Peter and the other apostles, "Brothers, what shall we do?" Peter replied, "Repent and be baptized, every one of you, in the name of Jesus Christ for the forgiveness of your sins. And you will receive the gift of the Holy Spirit.

Acts 2:37-38

Furthermore, in *Acts 16:30-33* we see that the same question - "what must I do to be saved" - was asked again. So, there is a something to be done in order to be saved. The scriptures answered the above by saying that in order to be saved you must believe in the Lord Jesus. The scripture tells us that after He has said this, He preached to them the word and after they accepted Jesus they were baptised. This also indicates that baptism is part of the salvation process. When we put together these commands for salvation, we realise that the scriptures are clear.

To be saved you have to **1. repent, 2. Believe, 3. be baptised and 4. receive the Holy Spirit**.

He then brought them out and asked, "Sirs, what must I do to be saved?" They replied, "Believe in the Lord Jesus, and you will be saved—you and your household." Then they spoke the word of the Lord to him and to all the others in his house. At that hour of the night the jailer took them and washed their wounds; then immediately he and all his household were baptized.

Acts 16:30-33

Romans 10:9-10 adds a fifth element which needs to be met for one to be saved. That fifth element is that you must confess with your mouth that Jesus is Lord. This means that you must truly believe this in your heart and so conclude. When you make this confession, that is your action, your faith. This also means that without one confessing that Jesus is Lord, He or she has not exercised their faith regarding salvation, which is a requirement for salvation. This also explains that belief in Christ is in one's heart and is something that a person must have concluded and settled on.

Adding this to our established conditions to being saved, it means that for one to be saved he or she must **1. Repent, 2. Believe, 3. Be Baptised, 4. Receive the Holy Spirit and 5. Confess with speaking that Jesus Christ Is Lord**.

That if thou shalt confess with thy mouth the Lord Jesus, and shalt believe in thine heart that God hath raised him from the dead, thou shalt be saved. For with the heart man believeth unto righteousness; and with the mouth confession is made unto salvation.

Romans 10:9-10

Ephesians 1:13-14 says that when they believed the message that they heard - as they accepted Christ as Lord - they were sealed with the Holy Spirit as a guarantee of their salvation. The scriptures above indicate to us that without the seal of the Holy Spirit, an individual's salvation is incomplete, and is not guaranteed. You need the seal of the Holy Spirit to guarantee your salvation. Therefore, receiving the Holy Spirit is part of the salvation process. You must make sure that you have the Holy Spirit.

And you also were included in Christ when you heard the message of truth, the gospel of your salvation. When you believed, you were marked in him with a seal, the promised Holy Spirit, who is a deposit guaranteeing our inheritance until the redemption of those who are God's possession—to the praise of his glory.

Ephesians 1:13-14

This scripture indicates that it is important to note that many people will believe in their hearts, will repent, confess and even be baptised but because they leave out the Holy Spirit there is no seal, thus indicating that you can wither away quickly, or fade away from salvation. In *Acts 19:2* they were asked if they had received the Holy Spirit since they believed and when they answered no, the Apostle Paul prayed and ministered to them and they received the Holy Spirit. The point I want you to know is that they were asked whether they had received the Holy Spirit since they believed, which means that after you believe you must make sure you receive the Holy Spirit. This also shows that, concerning the baptism of the Holy Spirit, it is not straight forward like confessing and baptising in water; there may be a time gap, yet you must, nevertheless, make sure that you receive the Holy Spirit; the seal that guarantees your salvation. If you have no guarantee, then it means your salvation is not complete; receiving the Holy Spirit is part of the salvation process. When you try to win souls for the Lord, the first thing you will learn is that you can save anyone and you can win any soul - for it is the work of the Holy Spirit. Your part is to present yourself and speak; to pray and to pray fervently. However, you will come to realise that you are just a tool and that it is the Holy Spirit who truly does the work.

and asked them, "Did you receive the Holy Spirit when you believed?" They answered, "No, we have not even heard that there is a Holy Spirit.

Acts 19:2

Colossians 2:6-7 which is connected to salvation and is about salvation tells us that just as we received Christ Jesus as Lord, just as we have been saved, we must now continue in Him. What does it mean if you do not continue in Him? You will not be planted, and you will not be rooted in Him and if you are not planted and rooted in Him, you will wither away. The continuity of salvation is very important because salvation is ongoing.

This is the sixth element needed for salvation. The scripture says to check yourself, to see whether you are still in the faith. We are to continue to walk in Him beyond the one time you repented, were baptised, confessed and received the Holy Spirit. Your walk must now be continued.

Remember that a Christian, a saved person or a disciple is one who follows the teaching of Christ. This also means to a continual obedience to Him.

So then, just as you received Christ Jesus as Lord, continue to live your lives in him, rooted and built up in him, strengthened in the faith as you were taught, and overflowing with thankfulness.

Colossians 2:6-7

From the above for one to be saved, become a Christian or disciple of Christ Jesus he or she must:

1. Repent

2. Believe

3. Be Baptised

4. Receive the Holy Spirit

5. Confess aloud that Jesus Christ Is Lord

6. Continue in his following of Jesus

ONCE SAVED FOREVER SAVED?

Satan is against salvation. Never forget that the number one priority for God and for the church is for our salvation. Satan has therefore made many schemes specifically to prevent saved people from remaining saved.

One of his main schemes against salvation is the teaching of 'once saved forever saved'. This is not true. Once saved is not forever saved. I have heard Christians saying that once saved forever saved because we are under grace. Again, this is not true. Common sense, wisdom and a clear heart will tell us that if it was 'once saved forever saved', this would not be right. If that was the case then once we are saved, we will simply go back to our old ways because we are saved and therefore, forever saved. Our conscience teaches us that it cannot be once saved forever saved so it is for us investigate the scriptures and find out if we truly are 'once saved forever saved.'

Matthew 24:12-13 writes that it is the one who is able to stand firm to the end that will be saved. So yes, it is evident that although you have been saved and you are saved now, your salvation will be determined at the end, because the end is what will define your status and whether you are indeed saved. Your end will be the state which you are found in when you die or when Christ returns whilst you are alive. So when you were baptised, you repented, confessed Jesus as your Lord and received the Holy Spirit, you were saved. However, this – your salvation - will be determined once you stand firm and remain saved till the end. We are *being saved* - it is ongoing.

Because of the increase of wickedness, the love of most will grow cold, but the one who stands firm to the end will be saved.

Matthew 24:12-13

Therefore *Philippians 2:12* says that you must continue to work out your salvation with fear and trembling. If it was a case of 'once saved forever saved' then the scripture would not say that I should continue to work out my salvation.

Therefore, my dear friends, as you have always obeyed—not only in my presence, but now much more in my absence—continue to work out your salvation with fear and trembling...

Philippians 2:12

Why did the scripture instruct us to continue to work out our salvation? It is because as of now we are saved, but we must continue to remain saved. So, if it really was 'once saved forever saved' then the scripture would not say that I should continue to work my salvation out.

Romans 13:11 says that our salvation is nearer than we first believed. In other words, our salvation is nearer now than when we were saved. Meaning, I am closer to my salvation than ever before because if say, I was saved 10 years ago, then that would make me 10 years closer to my salvation, so that if I stand firm, my salvation shall come at the end.

So now I am closer to it, I have already done 10 years! Even though I do not know that day, God does; that day shall come and I have already done ten years towards that day. If it was 'once saved forever saved' then that scripture would not say that we are closer to our salvation now than ever before.

And do this, understanding the present time: The hour has already come for you to wake up from your slumber, because our salvation is nearer now than when we first believed.

Romans 13:11

Just as diesel is not petrol, grace is not salvation - salvation is salvation. Mercy is not salvation, favour is not salvation, joy is not salvation, the gifts of the Spirit are not salvation and the Holy Spirit is not salvation. Only salvation is salvation!

Now salvation is a call and an election. We did not pay for our salvation, we were invited (called) and as we accepted the invitation we were chosen (elected) for salvation. Now *2 Peter 1:10* says that we must make every effort to confirm our call and election (salvation). How do you confirm your salvation? You have been chosen; you have been elected, but it must be confirmed at the end. The confirmation will depend on you, so the scripture says to make every effort to confirm it. So, we can truly see that it is not 'once saved forever saved'. *2 Corinthians 13:5* calls us to examine ourselves to see if we are still in the faith and therefore, if it was a case of 'once saved forever saved' the scriptures would not have asked us to test ourselves to find out if we are still in the faith.

Wherefore the rather, brethren, give diligence to make your calling and election sure: for if ye do these things, ye shall never fall:

2 Peter 1:10

Examine yourselves to see whether you are in the faith; test yourselves. Do you not realize that Christ Jesus is in you—unless, of course, you fail the test?

2 Corinthians 13:5

1 Corinthians 1:18 says that to us whom are being saved the message of the cross is the power of God unto us. The scriptures show that we are being saved. Going back to my previous example, 10 years ago I was saved, but now I am still being saved. I am walking in my salvation towards being saved. My salvation will come at the end as I walk in my salvation faithfully to the end. Why is the message a power to those who are being saved? Because salvation is not complete until the end.

For the message of the cross is foolishness to those who are perishing, but to us who are being saved it is the power of God.

1 Corinthians 1:18

In the parable of the 10 virgins, we see that they were all in the house but 5 went out of the house before the time (end) of the arrival of the Groom (The Lord). This parable too, presents a clear indication that the saying once saved is not forever saved. It is not the case at all, and it is a fallacy to think this way.

In Revelation 20:15 we read that anyone whose name was not in the book of life was sent to hell. It also means that those whose names were in the book of life would go to heaven. We know from the scriptures that the book of life contains only those whose names who are destined for heaven.

In *Revelation 3:5* Jesus said that He will not delete the names of the ones who are victorious from the book of life. What does this mean? It means that the names in the book of life can be deleted. Let us not forget that those whose names are in the book of life are those who are saved, therefore if one's name is deleted from the book of life it means that he or she is no more saved. If a saved person's name can be deleted from the book of life because of the inability to continue to the end, as the scripture says, then how can it be 'once saved forever saved'?

To say 'once saved forever saved' is to say that one's name can never be deleted from the book of life once it is written there and this contradicts the scriptures directly.

Anyone whose name was not found written in the book of life was thrown into the lake of fire.

Revelation 20:15

The one who is victorious will, like them, be dressed in white. I will never blot out the name of that person from the book of life, but will acknowledge that name before my Father and his angels.

Revelation 3:5

Once saved is not forever saved. I have been saved, I am being saved and my salvation shall come at the end. Till I have received my salvation it is not done because as *1 Timothy 1:19-20* says, I can make a shipwreck of my salvation. Therefore, the scripture says it must be worked out with fear and trembling.

holding on to faith and a good conscience, which some have rejected and so have suffered shipwreck with regard to the faith. Among them are Hymenaeus and Alexander, whom I have handed over to Satan to be taught not to blaspheme.

1 Timothy 1:19-20

The above scripture was specific; it said that they had suffered shipwreck regarding the faith (their salvation) because they were not able to hold on to the faith - that they rejected it. If they were able to hold on to the faith without rejecting it, they would not have suffered shipwreck. What does the phrase 'hold on' mean? Put simply, it means to continue. In other words, the above scripture is saying that for one not to make a shipwreck of their faith they must continue in their faith. Salvation is ongoing and if you are not saved you cannot even start, but once you are saved you must continue in it, a step at a time, one day at a time and it will come at the end. You will make it. No matter what, just keep going. Seven times you shall fall and seven times you shall rise, the Bible says. Continue, The Lord will help you.

The one who sins is the one who will die. The child will not share the guilt of the parent, nor will the parent share the guilt of the child. The righteousness of the righteous will be credited to them, and the wickedness of the wicked will be charged against them. "But if a wicked person turns away from all the sins they have committed and keeps all my decrees and does what is just and right, that person will surely live; they will not die. None of the offenses they have committed will be remembered against them. Because of the righteous things they have done, they will live. Do I take any pleasure in the death of the wicked? declares the Sovereign Lord. Rather, am I not pleased when they turn from their ways and live? "But if a righteous person turns from their righteousness and commits sin and does the same detestable things the wicked person does, will they live? None of the righteous things that person has done will be remembered. Because of the unfaithfulness they are guilty of and because of the sins they have committed, they will die.

Ezekiel 18:20-24

THE ATTITUDE ONE MUST HAVE REGARDING SALVATION

The reason why you must have a good attitude regarding salvation is because salvation is the greatest thing to achieve. Eternity is forever whilst this life is very short. Years ago, it was difficult to find testimonials of people who had visited heaven, but now it is very common because of YouTube. Search YouTube and you will realise that Heaven is a real place. Salvation is real.

In *Luke 13:22-28* Jesus was asked whether a few people would be saved, or many would be saved, and he directly answered that only a few would be. He explained that many will try to be saved but they will not be saved. He then made reference to the parable of the ten virgins saying that once the door is shut, many will stand outside and say in a summary "I was with you", in other words, I used to be (in Christ, in the church and was baptised) but He will reply back and say unto them that He does not know them; even though there was indeed a time and a season that they were saved, when the end came they were not found saved. So, He said many will try to enter but they will not be able to because by the time that the end comes many will no longer be in the faith. Salvation is not about what we were, it is about who we are now, other than that, no one will qualify.

Then Jesus went through the towns and villages, teaching as he made his way to Jerusalem. Someone asked him, "Lord, are only a few people going to be saved?" He said to them, "Make every effort to enter through the narrow door, because many, I tell you, will try to enter and will not be able to. Once the owner of the house gets up and closes the door, you will stand outside knocking and pleading, 'Sir, open the door for us.' "But he will answer, 'I don't know you or where you come from.' "Then you will say, 'We ate and drank with you, and you taught in our streets. "But he will reply, 'I don't know you or where you come from. Away from me, all you evildoers!' "There will be weeping there, and gnashing of teeth, when you see Abraham, Isaac and Jacob and all the prophets in the kingdom of God, but you yourselves thrown out.

Luke 13:22-28

Matthew 7:13-14 shows us why many will try to enter but not be able to enter. In other words, only a few will be saved and you can be amongst those few that are if you are careful not to watch what people are doing and try to be them in the church, but to instead look unto the Saviour, by looking into the Bible and obeying it. *Matthew 7* explains that the reason why few will be saved is because only a few find and enter the path and through the gates that lead to salvation and it is because this path is narrow, and the gate is small. It is harder, it is not popular, it does not look attractive; the gate is small, and the road is narrow. This is not because God wants only a few to be saved but only a few are choosing to walk down this way and through this gate. Many choose the wide gate and the broad path. They chose what is popular and comfortable for now and appears as freedom - to move and do as one please without restraint. However, if you want to have your way when it comes to salvation, then the narrow path and the small gate will be hard for you to walk on and go through. It takes humility to walk on the narrow path and to enter the small gate and sadly, many do not want to humble themselves before God in order to enter.

Enter through the narrow gate. For wide is the gate and broad is the road that leads to destruction, and many enter through it. But small is the gate and narrow the road that leads to life, and only a few find it.

Matthew 7:13-14

In *Mark 9:43-48* because of the importance of salvation, Jesus said that it is better to enter eternal life by cutting off our hands and by losing some parts of our bodies than to miss it and end up in hell. In other words, Jesus is saying that there should be no excuse to not make it to heaven or to not to be saved. This scripture also shows how important and precious salvation is. We are to ensure that nothing prevents us from being saved. Nothing or no one is worth preventing you from being saved. You must not allow anything to prevent you; if you are to cut of your hand or pluck out your eyes in order to be saved, then do so, because nothing should prevent you from attaining your salvation. This is not hard beloved.

Remember with God all things are possible and that which is impossible with man is possible with God.

And if thy hand offend thee, cut it off: it is better for thee to enter into life maimed, than having two hands to go into hell, into the fire that never shall be quenched: Where their worm dieth not, and the fire is not quenched. And if thy foot offend thee, cut it off: it is better for thee to enter halt into life, than having two feet to be cast into hell, into the fire that never shall be quenched: Where their worm dieth not, and the fire is not quenched. And if thine eye offend thee, pluck it out: it is better for thee to enter into the kingdom of God with one eye, than having two eyes to be cast into hell fire: Where their worm dieth not, and the fire is not quenched..

Mark 9:43-48

GOD BLESS YOU.

I WILL SEE YOU IN HEAVEN.

To accept Jesus Christ as your Lord and Saviour pray as follows:

Thank you God Almighty for sending Jesus Christ to die for me. I repent of all my sins and I ask that you forgive me of my sins. I denounce the world and satan and I accept Jesus Christ as my Lord and Saviour and confess that Jesus is the Son of God. Please write my name in the book of life and may it forever be in it. Thank you for your salvation in Jesus name I pray Amen.

Praise the Lord, you are now saved.

Look for a Bible and Holy Spirit filled church to join. May the Lord lead you to the church by His Holy Spirit.

Amen.

BOOKS BY APOSTLE E A ADJEI

Praying the Psalms

Manual of Practical Wisdom

Knowledge of the Secret

In the Words of The Master

Who is Jesus Christ of Nazareth?

Who is the Holy Spirit?

Water Baptism

Heaven as A Real Place

Speaking in Tongues

Salvation

Tithing

The Church

Printed in Poland
by Amazon Fulfillment
Poland Sp. z o.o., Wrocław